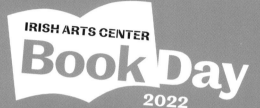

IRISH ARTS CENTER

Book Day
2022

THURSDAY, MARCH 17

in association with
**New York City Council
New York State Assembly
New York State Senate
ADL NY/NJ
Literature Ireland**

IRISHARTSCENTER.ORG | **#IACBOOKDAY**

THEATRE | MUSIC | DANCE | FILM | EXHIBITION | LITERATURE | HUMANITIES
CHILDREN'S EVENTS | EDUCATION | COMEDY | LANGUAGE

STRONG, MY LOVE

Peter Fallon

STRONG, MY LOVE

Gallery Books

Strong, My Love
is first published
simultaneously in paperback
and in a clothbound edition
on 14 May 2014.

The Gallery Press
Loughcrew
Oldcastle
County Meath
Ireland

www.gallerypress.com

ISBN 978 1 85235 593 7 *paperback*
        978 1 85235 594 4 *clothbound*

A CIP catalogue record for this book
is available from the British Library.

Contents

When the evening of this life comes
we shall be judged on love.

— St John of the Cross

Those who adhere to nature's laws are spared a fall;
no hunger brings them to their knees.
They'll have their fill at harvest homes. They'll reap
from earth a rich reward.
Their oak-heads swell with acorns; their oak-hearts swarm
with honeybees.

— Hesiod, *Deeds and Their Days*

for Alice and Adam

PART ONE

Always Something

There's always something —
a trail of bindweed
trumpeting September
the length of field wall
and worn fences; that clamp
of silage an ember

on the left as you leave here,
smouldering
on the slab
of Napers' yard on winter
mornings; a lace pattern
in the tractor cab

that's a dew-silvered
spider's web; new grass
a light veil of green mist
along the furrowed
brow of earth
it barely kissed:

a pledge of hay.
House martins on their lap
of honour around the house earn
our applause
as we concelebrate
the victory of their return.

Always something —
the hedgerow where
haw blossom simmered
and boiled over
in the heat of May; that smell
where honeysuckle shimmered

after a spill of rain. Spiders
perform high-wire acts
without a safety net.
A pheasant dives
into a pool of air.
Fireworks beget

ragwort's
rank alchemy of August
while manes of gossamer
wave in the currents
of low sky, windblown
on the horse of summer.

Crosshatch design
of elderberry bark
like harbour ropes in watery
sway — and all the while,
'way in the west, a trawler
marries port to sea,

the gulls' cheers in its wake
a bridal train
behind a sudsy wedding dress.
Always something . . . And now,
tell me again, who was it *exactly*
you were trying to impress.

Seven Waves: Inishlacken

Reeds rusted by December on the coast;
the clouds shunting their cargo of downpour;
a trawler nudges past a pier.
Seals haul their heavy weights ashore.

The arms of tides pounce to pocket
loose change of shingle.
It clatters through their fingers. An islandman
goes overseas to the mainland. A tingle

in the mist. A siren says, 'On land
dream sea', and he, 'Who spoke?'
Someone who said, 'I saw a score of ships and them
leaving the bay.' The sixth wave surged, then broke.

After a Storm

It took days
for the waves

to recover,
to re-form

their orderly queue
to land.

Then she said,
I'm not the better

of it yet,
and who knows when

I'll over it.
All I know is

I'm ownlier
than I ever thought.

He'd been
good as gold

the whole while
since, a shield

to ward off
blows of grief.

It's where we are
now, he said,

and these
are our lives,

as he looked
to the sea —

but a wave
to hand

simply shrugged,
then turned its back

on their separate selves.

A Thanksgiving

'Fête Day in a Cider Orchard, Normandy' (1878)
— William John Hennessy

As she thinks of his caress
she pushes tears from her eyes
and cries, 'Bad cess
to him and to the world' and 'Why's
there always such a price
to pay for happiness?'

Her sorrow and to spare.
'It was a thing of nothing,'
she heard him declare.
Until it grew.

Some said,
That's the way it ever was.
He takes all that he wants
and she's left with
all she doesn't.

⇒

Married, and not for love.
Everybody knew.
And knew
that's why he withdrew
and came back in a uniform.
But what could you
rely on? A game bird not to stray
or lay among long grasses
and the roots of vines?

⇒

As the children lay
untroubled by their futures
at a thanksgiving in Normandy
one evening when the rain
held off

she found among the shades
and fallen leaves a windfall —
and she rose
out of the dark of mercy
into its day.

A Winter Hymn

The snow melt falls
like footsteps
coming closer. You hesitate —
you hear your old friend's
'Old too early,
wise too late.'

You've learned his lesson.
He left it that there's not
too much to forgive.
You know the earth
abounds with benefits
and the chance to live

on it's a privilege.
In the bad year
good hay's
gold bullion in the bank.
As many as are
all the gone days

are beacons and bounties —
like the salmon
spawning in three
rivers in the city
for the first time
in a century.

As human as work is
in saw- and splitting it,
or 'winning' it, you feel
something divine
in wood and turf that warms
the family hearth, to which you kneel.

My friend says the mind of the honeybee
is a map of bloom.
It conjures lavish crops.
The ghost of winter snows
preserves a promise every February
in snowdrops.

Crane, 2

Beyond
where thistles and nettles and docks
and wildflowers rage
in that pageant staged
in the amphitheatre of everyday,

beyond
where sparrows and blackbirds and wrens
and robins raid
the hedge fund of grubs and berries, there,
where rockfall breaks the habits of waves,

mist ruffles the caws of gulls
and blurs the water's edge . . .
When you see a hawk
it's seen you,
but this smudge of smoke's

intent on further things.
A stillness become silence,
he holds us consigned
to hear the homilies of rain
with an autumn mind.

Who said that nothing is
but what is
now?
He proves we live
in different realms

and his lift-off
as he levers himself
on the fulcrum of air,
defying whims of the wind,
is a gift and grace and true uplift.

Let what remains of us
be our best part.
He knows responses
to the question mark
his perched body makes.

Commonwealth

for Paul Sullivan

The very day
sailboats
blossom on the Charles

magnolia blooms
unfurl
along the avenue.

The Weight of Wealth

after Tibullus,
Elegy 1.1 41-50

What would I do with,
    why would I wish for the weight
of all the wealth my people
    garnered in great

harvests? Enough for me
    a modest one for, if my whim's
indulged, I'm satisfied to lie
    in my own bed, and rest my limbs.

What's sweeter than to listen to
    ferocious gales that race
and crash outside, while I safeguard
    a woman in a firm embrace?

Or, while the south wind hurls
    its iced downpour,
to slumber undisturbed and safe
    before a fire's roar?

For this, for this I blissfully forgo
    my claim to any gain
to favour him who can endure
    the surging seas, the driving rain.

A Woman of the Fields (Revisit)

She studies herself
in the mirror
of all the men's stares,
a glimpse of spring
in winter's looking glass.

The way a wind grows
visible
on its move through mist
she charts
the geography of longing.

There's that report —
remember? —
of the woman who chased
the man so hard
he caught her!

Was that in a hayfield
or a haggard?
When you bend over
to pick up a pitchfork
someone left abandoned

at the last haymaking
new shoots of grass
compete for it.
Why veer towards
what will do harm to us,

the moth to flame,
the siren call,
the lemming to the precipice?
She pauses by a sign
in the rubble

of a marriage
and scours it —
'Find me. I'm lost' —
nurse, nightingale
or trouble.

And then, as though
the sky itself
were mis-
tletoe, does she bestow
her better kiss.

Late Sentinels

How would they know whether
they're coming or going
as they swish that way and this
in such fierce weather,

these winter trees between
the window and the lake,
those snappy ashes
and that steadfast evergreen,

its ivy clinging on for life?
The tips of Sitka spruces bend
like sailboats in a storm at sea.
Sturdy sceptres, emblems of strife.

Shrubs stand unshaken in the shelter
of an alcove, under eaves.
Late sentinels — their woodland
cousins flurry in a welter

of distress as when in fright
we start awake and worry
where we are. We scan the map
by lightning's light.

And so to whom now will we turn,
now that the long nights
lean on us? Now who or what
will guide us as they burn,

those fires of house and hearth,
in guttery flickers?
As if there were no end to plenty
we plundered earth.

Where are they now, those chaste priestesses
who tended embers borne from Troy
and kept them lighting year on year
for centuries? For anyone who transgresses

nothing worse than the shame —
not even the mandatory sentence,
for that became our task and duty. We had
their trust. They held us as protectors of the flame.

The Marriage Mine

May day. By hedges
of haw
and the hazel edges

of the wood
a busybody in the bushes
has withstood

an urge to fly,
a guardian angel
keeping an eye

on everything,
balancing that impulse
to abscond — or sing.

Our children's poise
at the point of take-off
deploys

the call to live another
life, mind the past,
hold still, and yet discover

re-entry to the kingdom
of what is
and what's to come.

Lead or follow,
deeper in woods
than birds dare go,

in shade or shine,
cleave to the word
to draw forth from the marriage mine.

Love Ties

after Tibullus,
Elegy 1.1 51-58

It's true, I'd far prefer
    to give up gold and precious stones
than have a girl greet my farewell
    with tears and sorrow's groans.

It's right that you, Messalla,
    contend on land and sea
so that your entryway may stay
    bedecked with spoils of war.
But the trammels of a lovely girl
    are apt to keep me
captive, and so I stand, a sentinel,
    by the threshold of her stubborn door.

Renown counts for nought with me
    if we, dear Delia, be one.
Let them brand me lazybones,
    the one who shirks what must be done.

Fish in the Sky

Roadside railings
on raised ground —
and you presume a river
but find no stream.
So you picture the bed
of a railway track.
Nor sign of that.
Nor padded path.
Nor passageway.

The heart of another
is a dark wood.
Now a woman comes to mind
who didn't care for me.
I loved her anyway.
And again that man
in a lea field
who says one thing
and means another . . .

As the main road gestures
anywhere —
a bridge over nothing,
a straddle of air.

Swifts

They know, it seems,
a kind of stage fright
as they delay and dither —
and no trial run —
each a neophyte

until it casts itself
and finds the palm of air
that cradles it
a helping hand,
a stair-

way it climbs back to heaven
where, an unstrung kite,
it sways
and slumbers on the breeze,
an acolyte

of tides' and seasons' turns
along the thoroughfare
of years.
They looked for sound
and found a prayer.

Like a duet with silence
their song an outcry of delight;
their being unearthed
in its fulfillment —
flight.

A Summer Flood

Again, I went out
to the new wood
because, at times as these,
it is a true good

to be alone
among the trees
I planted and trans-
planted, and an ease

among steadfast companions
to be one who believes
that answers can emerge
in leaves.

There was disquiet
in the house, a whirl-
wind in the ways and days
of our most lovely girl.

They stroked her like water
(that is, everywhere), the worries
and the woes, first deaths,
her teenage tragedies.

How live two lives,
of here and there?
(Wherever 'there' may be.)
May she pause (I make my prayer),

like salmon in the estuary —
our daughter —
acclimatizing
to fresh water

en route
towards a stay in gravelly mud
and waiting for
a summer flood

to tide them
over. Now contrails scratch
the sky. In June I watch
the mayfly hatch.

And then what had been
leafage in the night
began to ruffle
feathers, ready to take flight,

and birdsong happened
for me — no, for us
all — solo first,
then in chorus.

Law

Manhandled in the crush,
they'd bawl brute force against
the iron bars, gates at the gable end
of the stable row.   My uncle signalled
yonder. I climbed five bars beyond
harm's way. For now by law
they'd to be skulled. He came, all set
to work, with work coat and squat saw.
He took them on, one by one,
one side, then the other.
It was childhood shock and awe.

Shorthorn, Friesian, White Head,
Kerry Blue. Cut horns amassed
like battle trophies in the slush.
A sudden daub of powder on the round
rose of each wound. The snort
and grunt of pain. Each one an injured Abel
to our Cain.   And then that rush of blood
when he slashed through a vessel,
that pulsing arc that splashed
our hands and arms and faces —
and made muck blush.

          All brought back to me
by a footnote to the latest slaughter
in Iraq, where some of those that lived
envied some that didn't, in a photograph
a boy the age that I was then with half
a head, whose skull was shorn below the ear,
straight through bone. The gore coagulated
on a lack. And then I saw his hands were joined

as if in prayer and arms were chained
behind his back.
                    And Now met Then
when none of us was not bloodstained.

Thorn Wire

1

You've pile-driven the posts
the sledge would splinter or split.
You've fastened one end to the strainer
and unrolled and unravelled
the other eighty yards of it.

On the top of that run of sheep-fencing
you're stretching a single strand
when it unleashes its attack —
a coiled cobra springs, snags and rips
raw lumps from the back of your bare hand,

ungloved to grip wet staples.
I saw blood flow but had no feeling.
In the teeth of rain my crumpled palm
brimmed like stigmata. I saw bone,
an etch on it. Pain prospered on the bud of healing.

A stain on my smudged cheek,
across my jaw. Blood coursed the slope
of folded fingers and gleamed on brutal barbs.
Three decades on a scar remains, proud flesh
a badge of that skirmish with the devil's rope.

2

By the thorns
of the blackthorn
the black and blue
bruise of sloes;

by the thorns
of the quick-
the rosary beads
of bloodred haws;

like a tear
in the lifeline
on the palm of a land
a scar or score

the length of the front
and depth of the trenches
of a continent
at war

with itself.

3

'Cheaper than dirt . . .'
Devil's rope.
Burred wire.
'. . . and stronger than steel.'
Iron thistle.
Metal briar.

A thorn in the side —
to keep in
and keep out —
of the two sides
in the range wars —
a rout

for the tribes
that wandered
open spaces
with their lances
and skewed horses,
and for the other race's

herders and free-rangers.
All returned to me
that deer ground to a stand-
still, the insult
branded on its eyes
as the single strand

of rust
applied
its hurt and harm,

in woodland a remnant
of a fence that had outlived
its farm.

Sand
through our fingers
on plains and prairies;
on the wind's slow air
along a tensed wire string
lost lessons of the colonies.

4

While the women waited
counting the minutes,
hours and days,
and wondering if
they were widows yet
(and imaging the ways

they were, if they were),
their spouses waited
slowly too, like fish at low ebb
caught in a net, as they dashed
to escape, snagged on fence-wire,
butterflies in a spider's web.

There was in Buchenwald,
in a camp within a camp
where those impresarios
of torture strode, a cage
of razor wire, electrified, a lattice
pattern they referred to as 'the rose

garden', where they'd set
a prisoner all alone
to waste to death in full view
of his fellow men. An ensemble
played *études*. Bags of bones
that they were, what could they do?

Though like those who chose
to jump from the Towers (for surely they
couldn't save us now, the gods),

some opted for the sudden end
over the slow pyre — somewhere
a choir — to cheat death squads.

And this they named 'embracing the wire'.

5

Was there ever a moment
the fist of the age
wasn't raised and ready to strike?
In Indiana recently they found,
an aberrance of fate,
impaled on wire by a shrike —

the 'butcher bird' — the prey
it used to hang on thorns
(black-, quick-, rose), meat
to keep alive and fresh
and serve at will at intervals,
the nestlings' treat;

while in Missouri,
by a railway right-of-way,
out of scraps, a raven
shaped from broken pieces,
their spikes and spurs, a knotty snarl
for its nest, a harsh haven.

And further west,
where sides had seen
the range wars rage,
ten years ago a boy was pistol-
whipped and left for dead,
to finger beads of sage-

brush and the rough-hewn rail
they'd bound him to
with wire. He'd been roaming

for his kind of love, and been left, abandoned,
until a farmhand (who thought him a scarecrow)
slowed and found him, crucified in Laramie, WY.

6

Maybe he'd more wit
than the all of them together,
that Benjy, the 'idiot',
for when the Snopes boys showed
with their Texan prizes, mustangs on a tether

of wire, that stood unshod,
unbroken in a restive clump,
two score of them hitched one
to other and to the waggon,
snorting in stiff halters Lump

had fashioned of barbed steel
they inclined to hear his brother Flem's
'They're bound to be skittish
they ain't been rode in so long.
That's fuss and no fire. Them's

gentle ponies. In your heart of hearts
you know they'll settle . . .' — his frown
a threat — and they, with a hunger to serve,
believed what they wanted
and laid good money down.

Oh Rosa Bonheur, you'd seen
their neighs and snorts and whinnies flower
into feral fire at the fair, a whirl-
wind contained but about to explode
in the mane of horse power

that blazed like partridges
flushed back into the wild — oh Lord —

and for new owners the scant consoling
that out there, somewhere, in a torc of thorn wire,
they'd a horse, albeit a horse they couldn't afford.

7

Eight-gauge,
two-ply,
four-prong —
and miles,
miles
and more miles long.

And miles of it
within
each mile. Strand over strand
folded back one over
other, an aisle

or interval,
a stopgap in
No Man's Land —
a cut between
bloodstained strand
and bloody strand,

a stain along the trenches
from the English Channel
through the Eastern Front
to the cores
of families
that wore its brunt —

for no death is
to one;
from the Axis Powers

to the Allied Forces
the youth of different nations'
flowers

ripped to shreds,
their ribbons dangling
on those knots —
a fuse through the age's
powder keg — and at each spot
poppies as forget-me-nots.

A rosary
that shaded wars
along the wire century —
a blasted wick through time's
taper —
is known to me

by story and by memory,
by a scar's
small track
on the knuckle side
of my hand's
back,

my *right* hand's back;
and to anyone
along the 'last peace line
of Europe' — northern Cyprus,
southern Greece,
or the enclave of Palestine,

a whip of guilt
and greed, of those
we learned to know

so well,
from the open range
to the cages of Guantánamo,

all embraced by the devil's rope
and, now, by mild steel
galvanize, a chaplet curled
like a crown of thorns
around the temple
of the world.

An Outlook

They have ruffled
the embers of evening
and flap from its flames.
They come like clockwork,
minutes later every eventide,
a loud returning that proclaims

the row of limes in which
they pause, en route to roosting
in the rookery, a place of rest.
They sketch black scripture
in the sky. They watch
from trees where they don't nest —

these pairs and threes, tens
and dozens making thousands —
while I, intent on praise
and mesmerized, wonder what,
as they fly by, they might be
and realize: they are the days.

Field Mates

Now they lean against
a wall of air,
dozing.
Now they stand beside
the post-and-rail
fence enclosing

plantings and the paddock,
calmly smoking.
The birches shiver.
Like a knot of tide
unravelling
towards a shore a quiver

travelling the length
of Bella, to her black points.
The constant thrill
of seeing them wheel
to race: Bella the Mare,
Master Glow, Moses Hill.

Now they stand beside
each other, lips to hips,
muttering into the pile
of a muddied coat
their 'Scratch my back
and I'll . . .'

Horse power. Alert,
even at ease,
beneath a sudden halo

as though there always were
a way to snap the reins of gravity
that tether them — Master Glow,

Moses Hill, Bella the Mare.

A Winter Wound

Tears in his eyes
from an east wind
and ice rain
and, surely, more sinned

against than sinning,
he stared as the bullocks turned
back to confront a bare stall.
Had even the frosts not burned

the leaves from the briars . . .
In all the years that he remembers
there wasn't the like,
with its four Novembers

and the two or three
Januaries,
when any weather's switch
or swerve bore more adversaries.

I've known those nights,
up at the lambing, snowblind,
when you'd search for what
you hoped you wouldn't find.

I've seen those gaunt beasts
haunt the marts,
felt the heartsink
of false starts

in the low moans of live-
stock,
known the hurt hope
of herd and flock,

and heard his spirit say,
'This will not end,
not soon or in a time to come —
because it happened.'

The Two in It

1

When she,
after the serpent
struck, paled into the lower world
he, in the upper still,
launched his lament,

then ventured down
to her new realm.
'O deities of dark,
I beg of you,
this is too cruel a whelm.

'Spin again her destiny
and I'll remain
and not avail of my allotted time.'
Then to the strumming of his lyre
he issued his refrain.

Stopped in their tracks,
they stood — as never
once — in tears: Ixion, his wheel
at rest, in wonderment; Tantalus,
unreaching for his ever-

ebbing flow; even vultures
paused,
like creatures at an angelus,
from gnawing on the liver of Tityus.
Being overcome caused

Sisyphus to relax
his grapple on the rock —
and then they called to her,

those deities of dark,
and she came in shock

to witness them
backtrack
on the sentence that had been ordained
and say that she could go —
as long as she would not look back . . .

2

He'd have cursed himself
for his brief lapse and back-
ward look who,
caring for her wellbeing,
turned on that dim track

towards the light
and triggered her return
to depths and darkness,
who reached to touch her and be touched
and felt only the spurn

of his hands overfilled
with air.
And so he scorned all other women,
even she who was ashamed
of her desires, yet eager

to fulfil them,
and settled in a grove
with an upset no charm
or herb could overturn
to mourn for others and be a trove

of comfort, true companion
of all in distress.
There he composed
on his hollowed tortoiseshell
enchanting airs that might quiesce

the creatures of the wild
and drew
an audience of snakes
and beasts,
and maidens too

who flocked as birds flock
when they see
the bird of night abroad by day,
and they circled him,
beside encroaching rock and tree.

They charmed the winds,
those melodies,
and calmed the waves.
His strains renewed the strength
of oarsmen off in further seas.

Mortal, or divine,
there was no force immune.
Before, through lips to which
the stones attended, rapt,
and wild creatures comprehended, the tune

of his concluding breath
rang
out and melted with the breeze.
In that society of suffering
he sat, and sang.

A solace for both day
and morrow,
he shaped consoling songs
out of the shards
of his own sorrow.

(after Ovid)

The Man Who Never Was

You are taken
aback,
caught short,
off guard, by that near
quotidian attack

and he's there again
with you, the one
who never was a man;
still a brother,
still a son.

Is he his elder sibling's
unspoken
grief, you stop to wonder,
unmeasured loss,
who might have been journey's token?

Oh, would that it had been
that he could
reach up a hand
as that same brother did,
and sister would,

without a glance,
and know
that mine was there
to take it,
so that she might not be so

exposed, his mother,
in face of warning,
worn out already, her cross too much
to bear, nor need defer with her
'I'll hold him in the morning . . .'

Now I roll out
a dream
of him, his quirks and qualities,
a gift for this or that,
success on this team

or that, or none,
as I sit in wait
as if for something
to happen, but what that is
was fate

and has already come to pass
completely
and made the man who never was —
nor was a boy,
was but a fleeting baby —

who'd be a man who's twenty-three.

First Born

They have stashed
the seeds of light
to flourish
in the year's early surprise
as white

clusters of snow-
bells, votive fruit
dangling from
green stems around
the ancient root

of our sentry sycamore.
Their each head droops,
cowed by any frost,
but huddled in clumped companies
these shy troops

marshal
to surmount
the force of winter
from spring quarters,
their annual unfailing fount.

Fair maids of February,
bridesmaids
of Candlemas,
daystars in the sky
of now, their mute accolades

assert themselves as milk tears
or in pearls of joy.
Now I lie awake at night
and fret
about the boy,

the life in store
for him, his generation —
notwithstanding their capacities —
far from the land, driven
to distant cities' quiet desolation.

For the years (you learn)
don't come alone.
They bear their load
of apprehension, ache and loss,
the time of our lives' chaperone,

though lit they are by this
display,
for what once was first —
first loved, first lost, first born —
first will stay.

The Fields of Meath

From Crossakiel
the cairn's a nipple
on the breast
of *Sliabh na Caillí*,
the hill a fixed ripple

of Famine furrows.
I etched the map
of my life in the fields
that prop that peak.
I've suckled on that pap

for more nor thirty years.
I know that there are fields that heal
(though some find solace
by lake or sea or riverside),
if we but kneel.

The flower of Meath's
a withered bloom
eastwards across the county,
a scar extending through those lovely fields
manhandled to a tarmac tomb.

I've heard the homilies
of hawthorn hedges
in all weathers,
so all I learned in fields
and by fields' edges

I learned by heart.
For some those portals
are a passage
to another world,
resting place of the immortals.

Reared not far from here,
we heard of a report from Rusheen Hill,
a story of a fiddler
who vanished in a Tory hole.
Some say they hear his playing still.

Here, where I've been happy
and in my element,
those hawthorn strands
spanned lanes to snag
a hold of you in ways that meant

to say, You know and don't
forget, anywhere
away from here
is an utter
other where.

October. Afternoon. The walled
garden's grass still green
in a late carnival of growth.
Between Grennan Hill
and Mullaghmeen

the last light of day
reposes as it comes to us
down below
and grapples with the burden
of an inauspicious cumulus.

This is the home place
now. However far I go,
should I exclaim,
I know there'll be the compensations
of familiar accents in the echo.

A Far Cry

Let each step be a prayer
and not escape, even if you'd venture
to the far ends of the earth.
Dare to walk on air.

Chance turning a blind eye
to the present moment
and you might miss your proper life.
Be patient as the mare beneath her fly

mantilla. Be still in tender
times. Along the riverbank
dark birds extend their wings
in versions of surrender

and then, when they take
off, they soar. Heed their sermons.
Heed morning's constant benedictions,
winds' histories. Bend, don't break.

Credit that part of you
that hopes to be haunted
or lies submerged
like the three streams of Loughcrew

whose principles are graven
in your bone. Bear with this
Polonius — and trust the heart.
The heart's a haven.

You'll wonder if you're seeing
things as you awaken
to the need to dream
new maps into being.

Choose quietude. Don't shy from silence.
World needs be
no more than itself. Imagine.
Abjure the social violence

that has fractured families,
homes and hearts — we let go
the loved one, not the love —
and shattered whole communities.

Say never again to The Wild Irish Rover,
no more to The Minstrel Boy.
Give us back our sons and daughters.
Say that Ireland is over.

The Night Itself

The shoulders of the evergreens
stoop beneath the weight
of winter weather and bear
the woes of the world. Indoors
the tulips writhe in their cut state.

I look out at snow, each
of the flickering flakes
a living thing that ever was
as they incline towards earth's
impetus to goodness, despite its aches

and disappointments. Between
the bounty of hard won
retreat and the hardship
of a separation
from somewhere and someone

I was beside myself —
for we live in shadow,
scrabbling for that other thing,
the real. Whose shade is it?
That we might never know.

I'd favoured things
on a human scale,
the give and take of workers
with a crosscut saw,
the pitch fork, the square bale.

For there are times when time
itself is cruel — like that attack
at Flanders when a tank brigade
engaged with a battalion
on horseback

while their commander
posted from Front Lines
to the manager of his estates
concerns about the state
of crops and vines.

When my old friend
falters on a stair
or founders on a word or name
I see my fate, near or far —
who knows? — but there.

For at our time of day
the clock's determined tick
reiterates and reinforces
loss
in its monosyllabic

march. Are they, the keys
to our lives, in the future
or the past, as we breathe in,
breathe out, to weather
a storm and find a suture,

as we track a passage back
from unbelief
and come on wayside trees
transformed by morning's grace —
the bud, the leaf,

not to mention the bloom?
This season is a skeleton
to which Spring will cling. The threads
of dark adopt new twists and turns
until the night itself is spun.

A Woman of the Fields (Riverside)

Night of two moons.
Sky full of stars,
sequins on a Motown gown.
Two moons — the one
above, the other wavering,
settling down

in the riverbed. Once,
in the long ago
and waylaid
by another loss, we lay
together, your out-,
your every second breath played

along my upper arm
like fingertips.
The murmured sound
of pleasure in half-light;
we tended wounds in sacraments
of healing. We ground

delight from desire.
To see a place properly
you close your eyes.
Morning furred by fog,
the mountain loomed
in disguise.

There there was still time.
The birds translate a language
no one knows.
We hear it in grace notes,
a melody
moments compose.

You took your bearings
from the constellations. There were no
hard words to soften,
but the tyranny of time and miles.
You know who you are.
I think of you often.

Way Lit by Love

after Tibullus
Elegy 1.2 29-34

Whoever's way is lit by love
    it will be free from threat,
that path he'd sooner take;
    no ambush need prompt him to fret.

For me, protection from tormenting
    temperatures and strains
of winter nights; for me, protection from
    the scourges of torrential rains.

What harm, should Delia unbar
    her door, in suffering hardships
and she but mime an invitation
    with the motion of her fingertips.

The Then and Now

So little now and so much then —
her new address is Age, in Courage.
She has been leaving us since when.

Good woman and just citizen,
who mined the golden ore of courage.
So little now and so much then.

Her wisdom of four-score-and-ten
bypasses any rage in courage.
She has been leaving us since when.

Her children and her grandchildren
help her to scale the crag of courage.
So little now and so much then.

Her widowhood sustains a Zen-
like calm in the cage of courage.
She has been leaving us since when.

The word she'd say now is 'Amen',
epitome of grace in courage.
So little now and so much then.
She has been leaving us since when.

The Farther Shore

i.m. Tim Engelland 1950-2012

When you asked to see the home place
I led you to the pond we'd let go
every summer, where we'd net eels and fishes.

And they came streaming back to me, lit still,
the chestnut husks we'd fill with moss and paraffin,
ignite, and launch — a frail flotilla of our wishes.

Light (in the Sorrow Field)

She tilled and toiled
in her own sorrow field
and found that grief's a place
none knows till it's revealed

by entering it. That there'd be
joys of night
she stored the gems of waking hours
and prayed to see morning's delight.

A widow woman. Not like the bird
in constant fright
and flight from hawks by day
and owls by failing light,

she reckoned earth
and knew demise of cowslips
between hedgerow and silage strips
a preview of apocalypse.

What once were farms,
she'd say,
are now food factories.
Between hay-

and harvest-time
the wheels of years accelerate
till winter changes gears
and they capitulate.

More like the hare, field faring,
and following its holy orders
to lie low, true to form,
to be itself within the borders

of what's now, that she sees, through gate or gap,
and, though the wind cuts like a knife,
tells, Go, long lugged, long leggèd one,
run for fun, run for your life.

A Family Tie

She lit the candles
of kindness, one by one,
until her 'Pray for me'
and my unuttered
'I will mind you in the only state
time is safe, that is, memory'.

Your haunting by a younger self
tests a courage to keep faith
when so much disappears —
friends to age, the land itself.
The waves that weep on one lakeshore
leave the other wet with tears.

All that was long before I learned
(if I've learned anything)
because I read a sign
that any life might be
the same length as
a strand of twine.

Time, is it? Or time that's left?
The hours in which we partake
are but a trick
of retrospect and longing.
When you left home
it was *I* who was homesick.

Now what was and is
have separated, but are still twins
within that mystery
of time — or time and place,
as if a place
had but a single history.

For it was not a letting go,
no, more a series
of sheddings.
How often have I quoted her –
you can't dance
at all the weddings.

Now you chase your hearts
and aces the days bequeath
but brittle traces.
We might grow by healing.
Be strong, my love,
in the broken places.

I'd wake and want to give
the ordinary day
its due.
Who enters age amenably?
Who but a lucky few
complete their lives? It's true,

I'd seek the makings
of a summer
in a single swallow.
Do good work,
I'd tell myself,
and the rest will follow.

PART TWO

Ambarvalia (or, A Field Day)

after Tibullus
Elegy, 2.1 1-90

for Brian Friel

Quiet please, all of you.
          Now's the time to consecrate
the yields and fields in ways
          our people handed down.
Come to us, Bacchus, from whose
          manly horns grapes pendulate
in clusters, and Ceres too,
          who sports ears of corn as a crown.

By this day's sacred light
          let earth, the earth
itself, relax, the plowman too.
          In fact, upend the plow, let
labour be suspended. Unyoke the collar.
          Now in the pen that knows no dearth
of fodder let cattle stand at ease, each
          resplendent beneath a floral coronet.

Let everything be dedicated
          to god's cause.
Let no one contemplate
          a hand's turn to the drudgery
of work with wool. Be off,
          I bid you, pause —
and then steer clear of any altar
          who last night knew love's ecstasy.

The gods count as becoming
        purity. Come in unsullied clothes
and with scrubbed hands fetch
        water from the fountainhead.
Note how the sacrificial lamb draws near
        a shining altar followed by those
who process in white
        and in whose hair olive leaves are thread.

Gods of ours, that is our own,
        we scour the land and all
who dwell upon it. Drive all that's bad
        beyond our boundaries. Let no stem,
not to mention stack of corn,
        deceive a harvest with tall
spurts of growth. Nor have our ambling lambs
        be daunted by wolves that can outrun them.

Then in fine form and fettle
        a countryman will load
a roaring fireplace with firewood,
        his harvest hopes fulfilled,
and — a signal of his standing —
        a throng of slaves from his abode
from twigs and sprigs and bigger brush
        a model house, before his hearth, will build.

My prayers have fallen on kind ears.
        Hear how they spoke,
see how the entrails issued an auspicious
        message through the divine
emissary. Now bring forth a Falernian,
        long aged in smoke,
and crack it open so we can blend it
        with a cask of Chian wine.

Let wine add to the makings of the day.
    It's neither boast
nor real disgrace, being twisted on a feast.
    A stumble, a misstep or two's no shame.
But let whoever's drinking
    raise a toast,
'Messalla, hail', and in all that's said resound
    of he-who-can't-be-there the name.

Messalla, talk of the town,
    for conquering the tribes of Acquitaine,
you bring renown
    through your resounding victories
to those rough and ready ones, your own.
    Come here to me, while once again —
come here and help — while I repeat
    dues in song to farming deities.

Of countryside I sing, and country gods.
    Thanks
be to them as lords of that advance
    when man decided to abstain
from acorns as the cure for appetite.
    They pioneered the plan of placing planks
together and thatching humble houses
    with fresh foliage, a shield from rain.

And it was they (they say)
    who first broke
the bull and submitted him to toil
    and set the wheel below the cart. The annals
of wild ways shut down.
    Fruit trees took root, replacing oak,
and cultivated holdings throve
    guzzling waters from a grid of channels.

And it followed that the ocherous grapes
        squirted juice
when trampled underfoot and the unadulterated wine
        was tempered with clear
water from a spring. It's open fields
        produce
a yield of crops. A day the sun splits stones
        shears golden locks of corn each year.

In the land of spring the bee
        flits assiduously from flower
to flower to heap the honeycomb
        with sweet
nectar. And it was then, fed up with unrelenting
        work, the plower
first fashioned songs in dialect
        with a fixed beat.

Having eaten his fill, a shepherd plays
        in regular
time a tune on pipes of oaten straw
        to gods whose statues he enhances
with ornaments. Bacchus, it was a countryman,
        made up in blazing cinnabar
and with unpractised, awkward steps,
        first led the choral dances.

By proffering a gift, a prize worth
        talk about from the outset,
a buck goat, boss of his trip,
        he managed to subsidize his kitty's
meagre all. And a country boy contrived
        the first chaplet
of spring flowers and laid it on
        the household's ancient deities.

And from the country comes the ewe
    whose gleaming fleece
adds heft and heave to the load
    for dainty girls
and women's work, a whole worth of wool
    for spinning, the slow release
and steady hold, the to and fro
    of thumb and finger as the spindle twirls.

A woman weaving, buckled to
    her homespun
stint, celebrates her patroness, Minerva,
    and matches time with the earthenware's
rattling weight against the loom.
    It's said that Cupid, Venus' son,
came into being in a world of farms,
    kept animals and rampant mares.

And it was there he first kept practising
    his bowmanship, adjusting
and fine-tuning skills — oh my — he now has
    at his fingertips. Nor is his whim
to target animals, as heretofore.
    Now he delights in sticking
it into girls and laying waste
    the men who would stand up to him.

It's he who hobbles young men
    in their prime
and makes, before the doors of raging women,
    their elders bark
disgracefully. But he'll act as a guide
    for that girl who, at any time,
gives her guards the slip
    and heads towards her lover in the dark.

Her bare feet read the road
        like Braille
as she progresses through suspense;
        by touch her seeing fingers
find the way. Aye, they're piteous indeed,
        those whom the gods make frail
beneath such aches, while he's in bliss
        on whom good Love's breath lingers.

Love, come, our holy one,
        to our field day and feast.
But leave behind, we beg, your bow
        and far from here your blazing firebrand. Come
everyone to celebrate in song
        our fêted one, for each and every beast
make song out loud, but for your own
        poor selves sing dumb.

Or, should you wish, shout out loud —
        for the crowd's raucous din
and the bent, boxwood Trojan flute
        will drown out everything.
Besport yourselves while you can.
        Already Night is harnessing
fresh horses and golden stars
        are following
their mother's chariot in a merry dance,
        while in her wake, wrapped in
dark wings, comes silent Sleep,
        and nightmares too, on fumbling

    feet.

My Love, with Money

after Tibullus
Elegy 1.5 1-76

It's true, I've raved and ranted
     and boasted in a strop
that I'd be fine without you.
     First less,
now there's little of that bluff façade
     for I've become a spinning top
lashed on level ground by a boy
     with that skill only boys possess.

Turn and burn, rack and rake
     the beast I have become
that I desist from bragging.
     Consign
my ungoverned tongue to silence
     now and in the times to come.
But gently, please. I beg you on our secret love
     and when you lay your head by mine.

That time you were laid low
     and sick in sorrow's own
despondency it was my prayers
     and promises (as anyone retells)
that set you free. And it was I
     who purified with pure brimstone
the ground around you
     as the *cailleach* chanted her weird spells.

And it was I who took the care
     that no evil be done
by offering three times the seasoned spelt
     that dread nightmares not overpower

you. And it was I, too, who
        with my top undone and clothed in homespun
linen, tendered a novena to Trivia
        in the stillest, darkest hour.

I gave everything, paid all my dues.
        But it's another who
enjoys my lover's love.
        Reap what you sow?
He has the harvest of my prayers.
        Fool that I was to think if you
got well again there'd be the charmed
        life for me. Instead a god screamed, No.

I'll move to the country — with Delia
        as guardian of all we produce,
when the threshing floor
        and summer's sun put
grain aside from chaff, and she'll maintain
        in brimming vats our profuse
vintage, and must, those pale, glittering
        grapes pressed beneath a dashing foot.

She'll get used to counting cattle
        and to presiding, a host benign
to the houseborn slave so on a doting
        lady's lap a babbling baby rocks.
She'll learn the habit too
        of offerings to ensure the vine
is plump, of corn ears on the corn's behalf,
        a votive banquet on the flock's.

Let her take charge of
        and attend to everyone

while I — to be a thing of nothing
    in the house will me most please.
It's here that my Messalla will appear
    and here to him Delia will run
to pluck the sweetest produce
    from the pick of apple trees.

What's more, she'll mind so carefully
    this honoured personage
she'll both prepare and serve his banquet,
    a connoisseur of Xenia.
Such solemn vows I was lost in —
    but they're now shredded on the edge
of the four winds that scattered them across
    the scented wastelands of Armenia.

So often I have hoped to drown
    in drink my complete dose
of cares but, diluted by my tears
    of grief, my wines were taken.
And often with another in my arms —
    as I came close
to rapture — Venus admonished me about
    my mistress, and left me forsaken.

Then — her parting shot — that woman
    labelled me 'enthralled' —
the shame of it! — and claims my darling's versed
    in things that it's not fair
or proper to repeat. Not that she uses
    words for this: instead (though I'm appalled)
I'm captivated by her very countenance,
    a warm and welcoming embrace, her long blonde hair,

in just the way, once long ago,
    Thetis, blue-eyed sea goddess,
harnessed a dolphin like a horse
    and rode to Peleus in Thessaly.
With her paramour, a man of means,
    at home with her, I'll pay for this —
enticed as he is by a sly madam —
    it's going to be the ruin of me.

May all her meals be spoiled
    with blood. May the cup
from which she sups be red
    with bitter gore.
May erstwhile lovers swirl around
    deploring their misfortune while, up
on its roof-top perch,
    the screech owl starts its raging roar.

And may she, wracked with
    hunger pains, scratch
graves themselves for stalks of grass
    and search for bones to eat
ferocious wolves abandoned. May she race
    stark naked through the town before a batch
of feral dogs drives her away
    from places such as where roads meet.

So it will come to be. A god
    will send a sign.
If it's unfair the way she is forsaken,
    Venus flares. For anyone
who chooses love, there is a guiding light.
    At once, from that malign
soothsayer's selfish rule, take leave.
    Even love by bribes can be undone.

A man in need is always there
        for you. A man without races
to assist you. He'll cleave to you,
        an unremitting mainstay
by your side. A man without,
        true companion in the jostling spaces
will find a way to raise a hand
        to clear a passageway.

A man in need will escort
        you to meet your peers
in secret. He'll prostrate himself
        before his maiden
to undo the cords around her snow white feet.
        But, oh, our songs fall on deaf ears.
No door's unlocked by words. It's breached
        by the full force of a hand that's laden.

But you, who are now better placed than I,
        beware the fate that lay in store
for me. The wheel of fortune spins
        both day and night
capriciously. Even now — and not for nought —
        there's someone standing by her door.
He peers this way, then that,
        repeatedly, and then takes flight:

and acts as if he's heading home
        and then — like that! — the man
is back, all by himself, and on her step.
        He clears his throat
repeatedly. Who could say the ways
        of love. So, while you *can*,
don't waste a part of any day. On gentle tides
        your frail raft's afloat.

Author's Notes

page 10   Lines from Hesiod (230-233) from my translation.

page 23   See 'From the Crest', *New Collected Poems:* Wendell Berry (Counterpoint, 2012). I have treasured and been grateful for Wendell's work, example, support and friendship for more than thirty years.

page 27 *ff*   As did Ovid and Propertius, Tibullus (c. 55-19 BC) composed his poetry in 'elegiac couplets', that is an hexameter line followed by a shorter one. Whence his 'elegies', a reference to the form not to 'laments' as we understand the word. Delia was Tibullus's first love, Messalla his patron.

     I am again indebted to Michael Putnam for his expertise and for his generous encouragement of my translations.

page 34   The phrase 'fish in the sky' appears in *Walden* (1854), Chapter 2 ('Where I Lived, and What I Lived For'): 'Time is but the stream I go a-fishing in. I drink at it, but while I drink I see the sandy bottom and detect how shallow it is. Its thin current slides away, but eternity remains. I would drink deeper, fish in the sky, whose bottom is pebbly with stars.'

page 48   Rosa Bonheur 'The Horse Fair' (1853).

page 66   *Sliabh na Caillí*: The Hag's Mountain.

Acknowledgements

Grateful acknowledgement is due to the editors and publishers of the following, in which some of these poems, or versions of them, were published first: *A Conversation Piece: Poetry and Art* (eds. Adrian Rice and Angela Reid, National Museums and Galleries of Northern Ireland, 2002), *An Afterglow: A Gallery of Connemara Poems* (Occasional Press/Ballynahinch Castle Hotel, 2010), *Boston College Magazine, Boulevard Magenta, Boyne Berries, Captivating Brightness: Ballynahinch* (ed. Des Lally, Ballynahinch Castle Hotel, 2008), *The Clifden Anthology 35, A Fine Statement: An Irish Poets' Anthology* (ed. John McDonagh, Poolbeg, 2008), *The Fish Anthology 2009, Forty, From the Small Back Room: A Festschrift for Ciaran Carson* (Netherlea, 2008), *Honouring the Word: Celebrating Maurice Harmon on His Eightieth Birthday* (Salmon, 2010), *The Irish Times, Landmarks, La Paume Ouverte: A Festschrift for Françoise Connolly* (2010), *Marking Time, The Moth, Poetry Ireland Review, ROPES, Shine On: Irish Writers for Shine* (ed. Pat Boran, Dedalus, 2011) and *Twelve by Two for Terence Brown* (School of English, Trinity College Dublin, 2010).

'A Summer Flood' was published as a broadside for the Beall Poetry Festival at Baylor University, 2009. 'The Weight of Wealth' was published as a Goshen College Broadside in 2011.

Thanks, too, are due to LMFM, Lyric FM, Newstalk (Talking Books) and RTE (including Arts Tonight and Sunday Miscellany) for broadcasting several of these poems.

Much of this book was finished in the course of a spell at Boston College as Burns Library Visiting Scholar 2012-13. I thank Eileen and Brian Burns. I repeat thanks to Mary and Ed Downe.

I lost my two first readers before this book was complete. I thank them for their parts in it. I appreciate deeply the careful attention of my wife Jean and of Vona Groarke to the manuscript.